Need for Speed

Indy Cars

by Bizzy Harris

Bullfrog Books

Ideas for Parents and Teachers

Bullfrog Books let children practice reading informational text at the earliest reading levels. Repetition, familiar words, and photo labels support early readers.

Before Reading

- Discuss the cover photo. What does it tell them?
- Look at the picture glossary together. Read and discuss the words.

Read the Book

- "Walk" through the book and look at the photos. Let the child ask questions. Point out the photo labels.
- Read the book to the child, or have him or her read independently.

After Reading

- Prompt the child to think more. Ask: Wings keep Indy cars stable. Have you ever seen a car with wings?

Bullfrog Books are published by Jump!
5357 Penn Avenue South
Minneapolis, MN 55419
www.jumplibrary.com

Library of Congress Cataloging-in-Publication Data

Names: Harris, Bizzy, author.
Title: Indy cars / by Bizzy Harris.
Description: Minneapolis, MN: Jump!, Inc., 2023.
Series: Need for speed | Includes index.
Audience: Ages 5–8
Identifiers: LCCN 2021044336 (print)
LCCN 2021044337 (ebook)
ISBN 9781636906751 (hardcover)
ISBN 9781636906768 (paperback)
ISBN 9781636906775 (ebook)
Subjects: LCSH: Indy cars—Juvenile literature.
Automobiles, Racing—Juvenile literature.
Classification: LCC TL236 .H356 2023 (print)
LCC TL236 (ebook) | DDC 629.228—dc23
LC record available at
https://lccn.loc.gov/2021044336
LC ebook record available at
https://lccn.loc.gov/2021044337

Editor: Eliza Leahy
Designer: Emma Bersie

Photo Credits: Bruce Alan Bennett/Shutterstock, cover, 18, 23tr; Jon Nicholls Photography/Shutterstock, 1, 22; Droopydogajna/Dreamstime, 3; ZUMA/Alamy, 4; Tom Strattman/AP Images, 5; TO Race Photo/Alamy, 6–7; carroteater/Shutterstock, 8; Cal Sport Media/Alamy, 9; Jeremy Christensen/Shutterstock, 10–11, 23tl; Robert Laberge/Getty, 12–13; Grindstone Media Group/Shutterstock, 14–15, 23bl, 23br; HodagMedia/Shutterstock, 16–17; Danny Raustadt/Dreamstime, 19; Walter Arce/Dreamstime, 20–21; Sanit Fuangnakhon/Shutterstock, 24.

Printed in the United States of America at Corporate Graphics in North Mankato, Minnesota.

Table of Contents

Racing Laps

This is an Indy car.

It will race soon.

Drivers wear helmets.
They wear jumpsuits, too.

This driver wears gloves.

He sits in the cockpit.

cockpit
WAL★MART
Arai
COSWORTH

A green flag waves.

The race starts!

The Indy 500
is a big race.

Cars drive 200 laps
around the track!

track

road
I AM. CANADIAN
CANADIAN
CANADIAN
SONY
FedEx
GOLD #3 GRANDSTAND

Some Indy car races are on roads.

People watch!

Each car has two wings.
One is in the rear.
One is in the front.
They keep the car stable.

rear wing
front wing

DELPH
Safety Team
DELPH
Safety Team

Sometimes cars crash.
A pit crew helps.
The driver is OK.

This car makes a pit stop. A pit crew changes tires.

These races are long.
Cars need more gas.

AIM HIGH
USAF
PPG
AutoNation
SealMaster
MENARDS

The cars get back on the track.

Vroom!

Parts of an Indy Car

An Indy car's top speed is 236 miles (380 kilometers) per hour. Take a look at its parts!

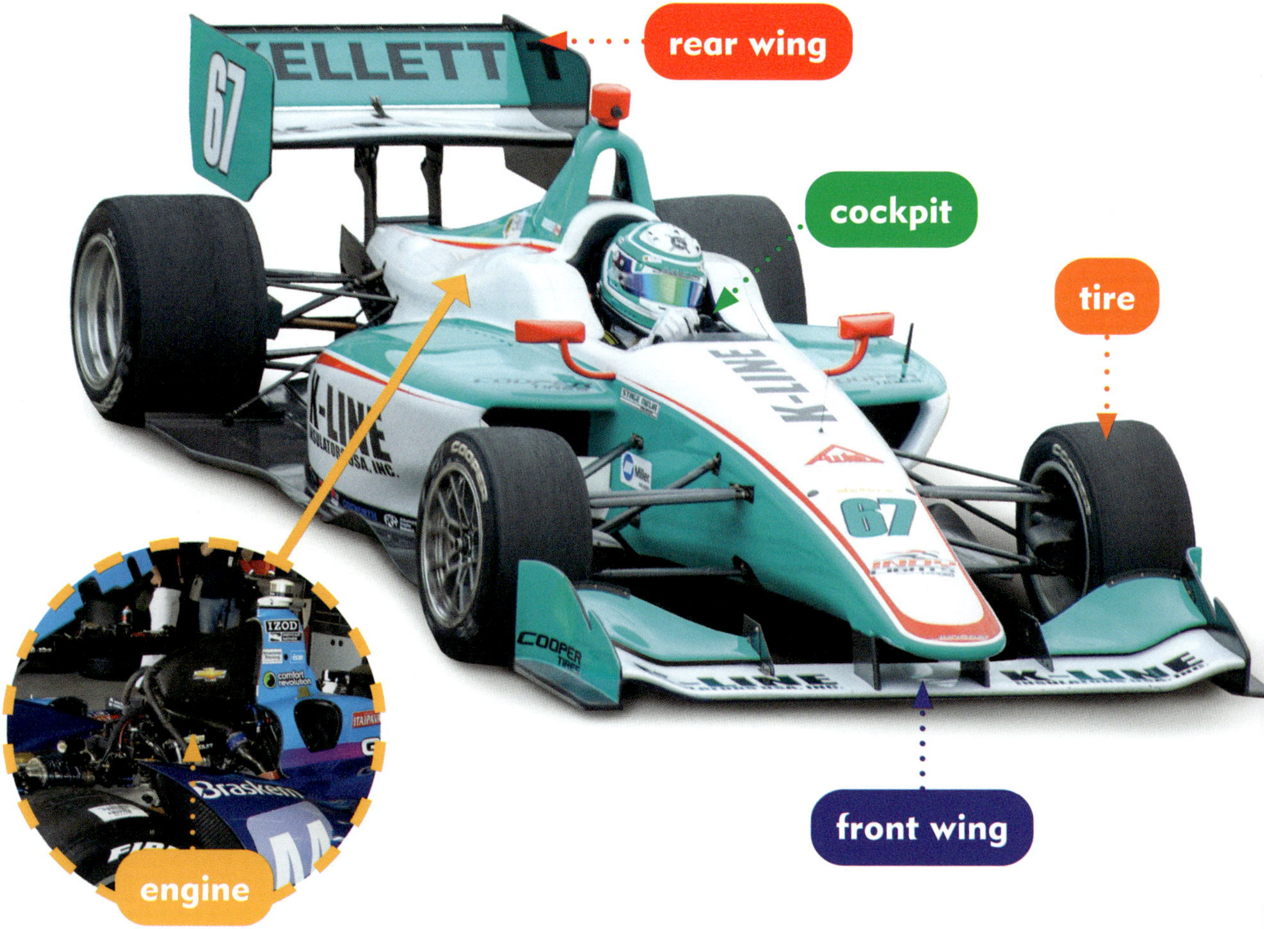

Picture Glossary

laps
Complete trips around something, such as a track.

pit crew
A group of people who fix a car during pit stops or after a car crashes.

rear
The back part of something.

stable
Steady and not easily moved.

Index

To Learn More

Finding more information is as easy as 1, 2, 3.

1. Go to www.factsurfer.com
2. Enter "Indycars" into the search box.
3. Choose your book to see a list of websites.